POEMS

BY

VINCENT O'SULLIVAN.

POEMS
BY VINCENT O'SULLIVAN

1896
ELKIN MATHEWS
LONDON

ᴥ CONTENTS.

❧POEMS❧

Go forth and find some fair pleasaunce (quoth he),
Some garden where no writhing serpents are;
For here reeds kiss the water wearily,
The moon is red, and from yon failing star
A poison-light falls thy sweet life to mar;
And little toads and gliding lizards thrive
In the damp grass, and keep grim thoughts alive.

The night is fading from the patient hills,
And night-clouds gather in your longing eyes,
O my pale love! while low the night-jar thrills.
And you would live, haste ere the cold night dies!
Ah God!—Cling close while yet a moment lies
In my weak grasp, and bathe in calm white fire,
And so be cleansed of lust and foul desire.

Then, sweet my friend, fare forth on rain-cool feet,
And joy with proud soft voice like rustling leaves:
But I the grey dawn must with sick eyes greet,
And try to love the thing that Love bereaves:
And hear dim music, such as one who grieves
O'er deeds of shame or some dark riven trust
Hears, and in pity watch my armour rust.

I THOUGHT the people's worthless praise to win,
Amid the gaping throngs to bear me proud;
I thought to hide my angry lust for sin,
And sneer my virtue at the vacant crowd:
    But in my sorry lot
(Who gazeth at himself must needs look low!)
    God was forgot.

God, Who has watched my ways with loving zeal:
Who once upon the cruel Jewry ground
Was wounded sore that He my crimes might heal,
And fell beneath His cross in bloody swound,
    Saw all my foolish aim,
(At which I wot Saint Mary's tears did flow!)
    And justice came.

In bed at night I sweat and shake from fear,
A devil sets me blazing with Hell-heat,
Ruin, Remorse, and Shame come edging near,
Their paces measured by my pulse's beat:
    Soon will my sin, now mute,
(Unless my God will turn aside the blow)
    Be all men's bruit.

O God, have pity in this desperate hour!
See in what grief my aching soul is tost:
Blind and a fool I was to doubt Thy power,
Ah, blind to join the army of the lost!
    Take now my life, my breath,
(If Thou wilt save because I sorrow so!)
    To serve till death.

THE KNIGHT OF DREAMS.

In the dusk church he watches at the altar,
And to the Sacred Host he bows his head;
Eager for God, he zealful cons the psalter,
And gauntly wails the litany of the dead.
And his white armour basks and glistens
In the moon's lurking beams:
While the hours throb for God's soft word he listens,
    The Knight of Dreams.

Or, riding forth upon a day in summer,
When sunshine dances gaily through the wind,
He hath a hail for every gentle comer,
And blessing for all folk of honest mind.
In low men's cause he clangs in joust and tourney,
His plume above the riot crests and creams:
He doth a deed for God on each day's journey,—
    The Knight of Dreams.

A sanctuary clothed in purple darkness,
And hearse-like dirges sobbing through the aisles:
Brown candles light a body in its starkness,
Black monks beg succour from the devil's wiles.
With the fair earth his steadfast feet have trod
To cover itself up his body seems,
In this last act of fealty to God:
    The Knight of Dreams.

3

When the moon is afloat,
And the ocean at rest,
The sea-elf goes forth
To the town he loves best:
Up from his cave, over the wave,
With joy in his breast.

Singing :   Sleep, little baby,
And dream on the sea,
That lulls round thy cradle,
And murmurs to thee.

The stars are a-shine
And the waves are at play,—
Rushing in to the shore
From the wind-stricken bay;
And the sea-elf is there, with the brine in his hair,
As merry as they.

Singing :   The soft fleecy moon
Is laughing with glee,
And soothing, my baby,
A dream-song to thee.

The sea-elf goes roving
When the moon waxes bright,
And plays in the church-yard
Till fadeth the light:
His morrice he paces, then deftly retraces
His steps through the night.

4

Singing :   Alack, it is gone !
The silvery moon,
With its great holy face
It waneth too soon :

Ere it passes, my baby,
A hymn it will croon,
Of the splendour of God
And the Heavenly noon.

LAMENT.

DEEP eyes that gathered laughter from the skies,
Thy cheeks of red-white roses bathed in dew,
The hands like cool quaint-fashioned ivories,
The spun-gold hair with sunbeams dallying through,
The cream and scarlet splendour of thy mouth,
And thy soft grace and dainty fragrance caught in the
      sweet South :

And now each charm has gone !—ah, now instead
Of thy slim self, lithe-limbed and strangely coy,
They shew this grey-white thing, this thing long dead,
With nerveless lips that ne'er have whispered joy :
That seemed so small what time we laid it down
In this hard bed, when all we wept was hair of tangled
      brown !

And yet my heart well knoweth it is thee,
Yea ! even knows the flowers which were thy feet,
And loves thee for thy death-cold purity,
And yearns to sleep with thee in slumber sweet :
Rest we together 'neath this drenched rose-bush,
Lulled by the little petals falling soft through the drowsy
      hush.

And we shall dream away the sultry hours,
Or sleep-flushed hark to small birds carolling ;
Our calm brows swathed in passionless hill-flowers
To shield us from the bees that whirr and sting ;
Thy thin hand slid in mine :—ah, lounge we there !
While low, faint music dies and trembles through the
      shimmering air.

6

BY THE SEA-WALL.

Wing thy race when the night comes down,
My cream-white bird with the scarlet mouth,
Fly to my dear in the sea-walled town,
Where she dreams her life in the soundless south :
Nestle thee close to her yearning breast
With a flutter of wings and a frightened stare,
And all the love-notes she loveth best
      Breathe there !   Breathe there !
My cream-white bird with the scarlet mouth.

Out from the fog on the cold sea-wall,
The death-witch comes with her ruined hands ;
The thread of her voice is thin and small,
Yet it whines afar over goodly lands !
God have thee in keeping, my cream-white bird,
My gentle queen lulled in love's mysteries,—
God help thee ! the tune of thy voice she has heard :
      She sees !   She sees !
The gaunt death-witch with the ruined hands.

She is weaving and weaving thy winding-sheet,
My beautiful love with the dreaming eyes ;
Her red tears fall and shall snare thy feet,
My passionate bird with the soft milk cries.
Her arm round thy musk-rose body she slips,
On thy face the grey sorrow of age is thrown ;
Her leering mouth brushes the dew from thy lips :
      My own !   My own !
My beautiful love with the dreaming eyes.

Like sheep that roam amongst the hills,
And ever press for richer grass,
And hear in each cold brook they pass
The splash of more delicious rills:

Or like the moor-fowl on the waste,
That joys in weary barrenness,—
Ah! mystic Queen, I sought Thee less
Than things which are my soul's distaste.

Strange scarlet things of sin and flame,
A housing in the home of sin;
From Thee to these I ached to win,
And hid Thy glory in my shame.

The sober grey, the calm austere,
Of gardens where still cloisters are,—
Dear God! this peace is sorely far
From me, nor can I gather near.

O gold Queen of the yellow moon,
Light up a little lamp for me,
With sweet prayers carven curiously,
That I may gain Thy presence soon,

And shake with wonder, like the priest
Who bends before the bread and wine,
And sees the aweful glory shine—
The white God of the Eucharist!

Mary! on green and silver morns
I see how this cool peace is won;
I see the anguish of Thy Son:
A haggard face, a crown of thorns.

A COLD NIGHT.

THE ice-blocks creak in the frozen weir,
A starved dog gnaws at an icy bone;
Here lies a sparrow dead, and here
A poor dead woman lies all alone:
Her stiff grey face is furrowed with scars,
And terribly stares at the cold steel stars:
The poor dead woman lies all alone.

The little old church is white with rime,
White and bright as a diamond stone;
In a thin clear note the bell strikes the time,
And the red cock crows in a drowsy tone.
When the pane is struck by the crystal moon,
The mother who lies by her babe will croon.
The poor dead woman lies all alone.

Over the fields, by hedge and tree,
A white thing comes from the frigid zone;
Chill are the hands of this gaunt lady,
Cold, grave-cold is her freezing moan.
See! to the corpse she doth softly creep,—
The wife of Death, and mother of Sleep:
The two dead women are all alone.

ROSE WITCHERY.

THE icy gems of dew
Cling to petals of the roses,
And the stars for kisses sue
In the moon-white garden's closes:
The fragrant dreams flowers hold, my sweet,
I sprinkle o'er your eyes ;
When roses with your roses meet
You bask in drowsed surprise.
     Sing low ! sing low !
     Rivers run cool
As they sigh through the meads to the sea:
     Sing low ! sing low !
     By the dim pool,
While the wind plays with leaves on the moss-rose tree.

The drops of laughing rain
In a rose's bosom hiding,
A scented silver chain
O'er your drooping lids go gliding:
A timid gaudy moth has thrust
Gold wings from roses' leaves,
And seals your eyes with pollen-dust
He glamorously thieves.
     Sing low ! sing low !
     Balm is thy breath
As it sweetens the roses with mysteries of thee:
     Weep low! weep low !
     Balm too is death,
In a grave at the foot of the moss-rose tree.

THE LADY.

Now, as he listens to the purring noise
Of words she soothes to guests who linger late
When the lights pale, that they may yet rejoice
In the dear sounds which their souls perturbate :
Alas ! (he thinks), must this soft satin voice
      In the death-rattle grate ?

And when he feels the glamour of her laugh,
Her red mouth, and her teeth,—he tries to shun
Her mocking eyes, and heedless of her chaff,
Thinks how these teeth will rot out one by one,
Under a stone which bears her epitaph,
      Far from the silver sun.

The small white hands she nurses with such care,
While bracelets and old rings their charms confirm,
Ah ! lover's kisses have but little share—
But little share and for a little term,
In the atrocious meal she doth prepare :
      Food for the slimy worm.

Great God ! he knows that blighting day is near,
A day he often lives in monstrous dreams,
When, in a house where servants move in fear,
And dark men come, while some wretch sobs and
      screams,
'Mid stifling flowers he shall stand by her bier,
      And think how old she seems.

PIRATE-WIFE'S SONG.

OUT from the shore the men sail away,
(But thou must sleep, my woolly cushee!)
Sail with a cheer from the green-walled bay,
To catch the spell of the laughing sea.
They sail in search of the merchants old
Who travel the ocean with bags of gold,
And fine goods win by their greed and sin:
(But thou must sleep, my woolly cushee!)

As the ship groans on through the lonely night,
(Nestle down warm, my woolly cushee!)
On our starboard bow glints a small red light,
And those cunning old merchants do scuttle and flee!
But our ship is fast and we crowd on sail,
And we ride them down in the screaming gale;
For we've babes to keep who are sound asleep:
(Nestle down warm, my woolly cushee!)

Out of the hold those old men we drag;
(Laugh in thy slumber, my woolly cushee!)
They are sore afraid of our proud black flag,
As it flaps and veers on the dark cross-tree.
On the quarter-deck we muster a rank,
And into the waves we run a plank:
There are too many wails on the sea to tell tales:—
Come to thy mother, my woolly cushee!

WHITE DREAMING.

AND look with terror on the flat white bay;
On small ships tacking for the northern sea,
That from the holding green waves shake them free:
Ah! dull I stare till sun-down seals the day,
And pray God that your voice may reach this shore
      Once more, once more.

Please cry yet once: I hear not for the noise:
The storm-birds shriek, the wind is on the marsh,
And ruffles it with iron words and harsh,
And I am near too dull to catch your voice,
Dear love, dead love, and you lie down so deep!
      Call that you sleep.

The fog sighs in with clammy silent feet,
Then on the ocean walk the poor grey ghosts:
Hear now the dry wails from the shaking hosts,
Hear one thin wail the other wailers greet:
Sweet friend, 'tis you! no warmth is in your breath—
      No warmth, but death.

Oh, how I fought to catch you from the rain
That kissed your face and woo'd you far from home;
To hold you from the haughty dancing foam,
And take myself the anguish of your pain!
Alas! the sea thuds and the large gull screams.
      Dreams, dreams—all dreams.

At length has come the twilight dim,
The sun has set, the day has died;
And now we sing Thy holy hymn,
O Mary maid, at eventide.

To Jewry, to that far-off land,
Erstwhile there came a little child:
You led Him softly by the hand,
He was so very small and mild.

Like us, He could not find his way,
Although He was Our Lord, the King:
And so we beg we may not stray,
Nor do a sad or foolish thing.

Teach us the prayer that Jesus said,
The words You sang and murmured low,
When He was in His tiny bed,
And all the earth was dark and slow.

Hushed are the trees, and the small wise bees,
Our fathers are on the deep,—
Little Mother, be good to us, please!
It is time to go asleep.

Honour unto High God most sweet,
To Christ, Saint Mary's Son,
And to the Ghost of God, is meet,
Until our race be run.
      Amen.

ARIADNE.

ONE great star that lamps the night
Breathes reproach upon my strife;
Its calm gleaming sets me dreaming
All the evenings of my life,
    Ariadne!
Oh, its stillness sets me dreaming
Of thy soul that walks its gleaming:
    Ariadne! Ariadne!

Were the saints that walk in white
In the Silver Courts of Heaven,
More adoring of you soaring—
Was Our Lord's love greater even,
    Ariadne,
Than the love of one poor clod,
Who by this crept nearer God?—
    Ariadne! Ariadne!

Ah, last year was draped in darkness,
But last year, thank God, is dumb!
It was only one less lonely
Than the yearning years to come,
    Ariadne;
And I look a-down these years
Shuddering and blind with tears—
    Ariadne! . . . Ariadne! . . .

PAPILLONS DU PAVÉ.

A BUTTERFLY, a queer red thing,
Comes drifting idly down the street:
Ah, do not now the cool leaves swing,
That you must brave the city's heat?

A butterfly, a poet vain,
Whose life is weeping in his mind,
And all the dreaming of his brain
Is blighted by the dusty wind.

A painted butterfly sits there,
Who sickens of the *café* chaff;
And down the sultry evening air
She flings her sudden weary laugh.

God our Father, to the splendour of Thy mercy grave
  and tender,
    He who saddened, greatly gladdened,
    Now his puny praise doth render ;—
    Chaunting with the legions thunderous
    To the God obscure and wonderous
All the carols that his false mouth used before to sing
  to crime :
    Of the passions in his breast
    Which outflamed and murdered rest,
Lo ! the chars are pieced together and by Thee are
  made sublime.

O Lord Jesus, all Thy grieving when my foul soul
  thou wast leaving,
    Thy distressed state for an ingrate
    Who from Devil's purse was thieving,
    Thy dear mercies sweetly lighting
    In my soul dark sin was blighting,
Leave me blinded, dazed, and stricken from the fulgent
  skiey blast !
    By the sweet power of Thy pity
    Thou hast brought me to Thy city :
Broken, spent, and all unarmoured, yet I stand Thy
  knight at last.

Holy Spirit, Who didst press me to Thy service and
       confess me,
    From Thy breathing I am wreathing
    Scented flowers with which to dress me:
    In my mad and fitful dreaming,
    Thy soft grace was ever beaming
To lighten up the path which had become so dark and
       lonely:
    And oh, Great Mystic Ghost!
    Let me join the quiring Host,
That trembles at the awfulness of living for Thee only.

TWO VOICES.

The apples dropping from the trees,
A smell of apples in the air,
As I lay in the orchard there,
And drowsed amid the humming bees.

The calm sun of the afternoon
Was silver on the mountain top;
The restless white hour seemed to stop,
While o'er the mountains dreamed the moon.

In some field near the sad-eyed cows
Just move and shake their little bells:
The friars come from their lonely cells,
And each one to the altar bows.

Through convent casements opened wide
There floats the praise of Holy God;—
Of Jesus Christ Who our earth trod:
The God Who lives, the God Who died.

Away! away! soft earth-voice flee!
My heart is sick, my brain is fire:
Why am I not in that cold quire?
Why am I what I would not be?

The mist creeps up with whispering feet,
The whole fair scene is shrouded in;
Save where a ghastly scarlet sin
Takes stand my sullen night to greet.

DIRGE.

On the hillside where the sun shines brightest,
   And the fairest wild flowers grow,
On the hillside where the rain falls lightest,
   And the soft sea-breezes blow:
     There lay her low,
     To sleep, to sleep.

Up the ocean-roads on a fine afternoon,
   Blows a strong sea-wind from the west ;
But for her no sound save the bee's low croon,
   And the rustle of a harebell's crest :
     So let her rest !
     To sleep, to sleep.

All the rough and boisterous weather,
   All the groaning of the trees,
To keep quite still have vowed together,
   So that she may have ease,
     And rest in peace :
     To sleep, to sleep.

She cannot hear the skylark's trill,
   The shouts of girls and boys,
The plashing brook, the creaking mill,—
   She hears not any noise,
     Save one sad voice :
     To sleep, to sleep.

BRAIN FEVER.

THE garden in the sunset glow
Lies proud and breathing faintly sweet,
While pale leaves through the windows blow,
And roses wither in the heat.

The piled-up clouds have caught a ray
And buried it within their breasts:
The last kiss of the failing day,
When the day sighs before it rests.

Yet towards the ocean still I lean,
Filled with vague dread and ill at ease;
I fear that rolling eye of green,
The oily splash of summer seas.

A ship sails over to the clouds,
And now her sails are bathed in red;
A strange ship!—for her sails are shrouds,
Her hull the four planks of the dead.

A passenger upon the deck
Whose queer familiar face I scan:
Who is he, this derided wreck
Of life, this weary broken man?

I wave to him, and hotly strain
To let my glance fall in his eyes;
Why does he bring me all this pain—
This old friend in a new disguise?

He shudders: it is growing late:
He lifts his face and looks above:
He shews a face I scorn and hate,
He shews a face I wildly love.

Horror! this hateful face I know!
It is *Myself* I hail and greet,
While pale leaves through the windows blow,
And roses wither in the heat.

IN WINDOW-LIGHTS.

From Thy pure hands upon the restless sea
   Grace flows in silver streams ;
In the white rays old thoughts come back to me,—
     Like one who dreams,
     When each thing seems
   Fashioned in harmony.

Old thoughts, my Mother, of an olden time
   Before the Sacred Host :
Before the Father and the Son Sublime
     And Holy Ghost
     I bowed, almost
   Free from the stains of crime.

Before Thee, Mother dear, my little cares
   And sins no more I felt :
My Angel Guardian to the devil's snares
     A mighty death-blow dealt,
     And near me knelt
   To teach me all my prayers.

The sunlight creeping through the coloured pane
   In purple, gold, and red,
Seemed like the brilliant crown which Thou wert fain
     To place upon my head,
     When I was dead,
   And in God's peace did reign.

To-day I come without one prayer or psalm :
   My weak tormented soul
Can win no crown, can gain no palm :
     Dark knellers knoll
     Thy tranquil goal,
   And God's great holy calm.

23

SEA-SOUNDS.

HIDE your sweet face in the pillow,
My dear warm lamb, my gentle son:
Fairies on the silver billow
Dance and sing till night is done,—
Laughing till the night is done!
Oh, so softly they come peeping
At your crib, my darling one!
Hushaby, my baby sleeping.

I hear the drowsy breezes humming
Round the father's ship at sea,
And he tells them he is coming—
Coming back to you and me:
Bring him safely back to me,
Jesus!—from the cruel creeping
Mist and frost-rain keep him free:
Hushaby, my baby sleeping.

Oh, my child, when you are older,
And at night you set the sail,
May no harsh wind strike you colder
Carrying by a hopeless wail:
A woman's cry, a low sad wail,
A shuddering sound of awful weeping,
Or a dead wife's ghostly hail!—
Hush thee, hush, my baby sleeping.

CAITIFF'S RHYME.

One last message ere I rest
    I must send,
One word torn from my breast
    At the end ;
'Tis the last and so the best,
    Sweet my friend !

That in Heaven I only see
    Livid blue,
No one on the earth is free,
    Nothing true ;
God himself is naught to me—
    Wanting you.

In the agony of to-morrow
    (When I die)
One full breath from life I'll borrow,
    One hot sigh,
To curse the man who brought you sorrow,—
    Even I.

FAIRY MUSIC.

I.

Trip it deft and merrily,
On a sward of moonlit green,
Dancing blithe and cheerily,
Sipping drops of dew between:
      Hola! Hola!
      Ha! ha! ha!
How the funny white stars twinkle
Looking at the fairies' feast;
Haste thee, haste thee, blossoms sprinkle
Ere a stain comes in the East:
      Hola! Hola! Hola!

II.

When the calm earth the sunlight misses,
In the coolness of midnight hours,
We come with our laughter and kisses,
Bringing new scents to the flowers;—
Bringing sweet smells to the pretty field-bells,
And soft scents to the dear little flowers.

For we light on a rose and a lily,
And we fondle and kiss till they swoon;
Then we breathe with breaths fragrant and chilly
We have caught from the streams of the moon;
And we whisper them stories of crystalline glories,—
Being sick with our love for the moon.

26

III

Cheep, cheep,
Birdie asleep!
I'm sure I won't hurt you,
But indeed I must peep!
So I lift up the straw
And pop my head in,
And then I say "caw!"
And you wake at the din:
For you think 'tis the rook
Who, the bird mothers say,
Brings bad birdies to book
'Twixt the night and the day.
But I'm not going to take you,
Ssh! Ssh! in your nest,
And of course I won't wake you,
For birdies need rest.

Hush thee, little cosset, hush and fear us not,
And up the path of star-light with the fairies ride;
And thou shalt have a golden lily for thy cot,
And a coverlet of gossamer and dew beside.
Thy pretty fairy mother,
Watching for thy other,
Will kiss thee and will play games with thy funny little
toes!
Hush thee, little cosset, hush and fear us not,
And we shall keep thee warm when the north wind
blows.

V

Eleuthera! Eleuthera!
By the water we have sought her,
For the mild night wanes and dies;
She is lost—our fairest daughter,
And the woods repeat our cries:
Eleuthera! Eleuthera!

A lizard gave her pretty timid fright,
And then she fled—he scared her so!
Her raiment was cut from the mellow moonlight,
And her vesture was made of a deep rainbow.
     Eleuthera! Eleuthera!

Come, our pride with meadow-eyes,
Mortal guerdons soon decay;
Soon the heavy sun will rise,
And we must away! away!

Let us feel thy grass-cool limbs,
Ere the blatant cock doth crow,
Ere the priests intone their hymns,
Or milkmaids to the dairy go.

The night is failing, failing,
Our voices sound afar,
We watch with sombre wailing
The death of the last star. . . . .
  *   *   *   *   *
     Eleuthera! Eleuthera!

OLD MOTHER'S LULL-TO-SLEEP.

THE little lambs are drowsy and the little birds are
      blinking,
And the lovely little fishes are a-sleeping in the sea ;
Already in the sky I see three little stars are winking,
And I know a little girl who is sleepy as can be.

    So sleep, sleep, pink bird Aline,
    And dream that you are a wee fairy queen,
    With dancing sprites
    And other dear mites,
While the night flits away and the white moon shines.

Up the stairs and to your room comes your mother
      softly stealing,
And she softly lies beside you in your snug and cosy
      bed :
Two tired little hands her sweet gentle face are feeling,
And on her arm is resting now a tired little head.

    So sleep, sleep, my love Aline,
    And dream of the prettiest horse ever seen !
    It lingereth not
    And you gallop and trot,
While the night flits away and the white moon shines.

To-morrow when the sun is warm will be time for
      playing
With the pretty coloured shells and tiny laughing
      waves ;

But to-night you must find out what the jolly men are
   saying,
Who live beneath the ocean in their shining crystal
   caves.

   So sleep, sleep, soft dove Aline,
   And be sure that you tell us what wonders have
      been,
   And what say the elves
   When they're all by themselves,
While the night flits away and the white moon shines.

A TRIUMPH.

ALTHOUGH I part in dreaming wise,
And you have slaves beneath your heel,
Can you still think I do not feel
The sad strange languor of your eyes?

Eyes that sing of wild strong ways,
And of sweet days that ne'er have died,—
When you and I our love strength tried,
And lightly scoffed at yesterdays.

But then our Lord leapt forth from thunder,
And He cried clear a-down the Heaven:
" I will to save this mean man even,
Yea, he shall see My grace and wonder ! "

And so at length I recognize
God's soft calm mercy in bestowing
The splendent graces flowing, flowing,
From the grace within His eyes.

Now sore a-tremble and afraid,
I twist and mouth the word Farewell:
You shall not know my hermit's cell,
Nor e'en the grave where I am laid.

And yet you sure would follow me,
And yield our soiled and worn behaviour,
If I were only Christ our Saviour,
And you were only pure and free.

Before Thy coming I fall down,
High God in Whom all worlds meet:
Let me draw near and feel Thy feet,
And bite the dust cast from Thy gown.

HERMIT'S HARROW.

THE lights flared and flashed as she entered the hall,
She bowed to the almoner and seneschal,
She smiled at her dames and her pages withal,
    But her eyes never turned to me.
    Fair as twin lilies her hands
    Holding the Queen's rosary,
       And the light,
       Not so bright
    As her glorious hair,
Sought her head and dwelt there.
I chaunted my mad minstrelsy,
Caught from the wind as it cried to the sea:
Wild was the wind and it whitened the sea.
    (*Jesus, our Saviour, have mercy on me!*)
I sang while the tempest drove in through the door,
While the hinds drained the wine-cups and shouted for
    more,—
And my song was of ships on a desolate shore.
     *   *   *   *   *
(*Whence is this night-wrack and where is the day?*
    Stainless Maid Marie, Thy pardon I pray.)

    I grasped a rich flagon
    And knelt before her,
    Where she sat with her maids
    In an odour of myrrh.

"Drink!" I cried, "here is the end of all craving;
Here is the balm of hot rancour and raving;

Here in this bowl is life's sweetness and saving ! "
(*Oh, the wind it came sighing up from the grey sea!*)

The roar of waves lashing the sands,
The shrieks of the fiend of the flood ;—
And the red wine splashed over my hands
With the wetness and glare of new blood.
Then, *then* she smiled and she drank of the wine ;
I played and I sang, for revenge is no crime :
Black was the poison enclosed in the bowl :
Jesu ! have pity on my blacker soul.
   Fair was she!

NIGHT VOYAGING.

In the last soft breath of the dying day,
When flowers are hushed, and the sun goes down,
Take my hand, dear child, and we'll wander away
To the noiseless wharves of the grey old town.
Here are the vessels *God's Gift* and *Heart-ease*,
But the fair ship *Dream-land* I think is best;
From her rigging falls sweetly the song of the breeze:
Sleep, little baby, the tired must rest.

Let us enter the ship, for the sails are set
To bear us full many a mile from here:
We are leaving astern grim doubt and regret,
And the funny brown sailors right lustily cheer!
Through the wan still moonlight we gently glide,
Pleasantly rocked on the sad sea's breast,
While the small waves whisper and splash on the side:
Sleep, little baby, the tired must rest.

And for miles and miles through the star-sown night,
O'er the purple seas that the fairies know:
When, alas! outflashes the morning light,
And sighing we land at the tidal flow.
But the folk we think in the churchyard lie
Sail on and on to the golden west:
They *never* return—yet why should we cry?—
For, dear little baby, the tired must rest.

THE CATHEDRAL.

In the old Picard city lashed with rain,
One passeth slowly through the narrow streets,
While the grey twilight with the nightfall meets
And leaves a strange anxiety and pain,—
Which when defeated rushes back again,
And clings still closer after sore defeats,—
Until this aweful church his sad eye greets,
Shewing so fresh and young 'neath Time's harsh stain.

Above the town thou dost sublimely stand
Century-defying! Who would now unfold
Man's petty ills before man's mighty hand!
Over thy towers have monstrous evils rolled
And scatheless left thee: solitary, grand,
A wondrous triumph magnificently old.

I KNOW not where this gloomy road will bend,
What foes will come, nor when my march will end:
    The night is cold and dark,
  And I have none to call me friend.

Even the screech-owls to their eyries fly:
'Mid the rank wayside plants I faint,—I die
    From poison-breath,—when hark!
  Across the land a low, deep cry.

"My poor sad son, dost thou forget the years
I strove to gain thee with My wounds and tears,
    And walk thine own wild road
  Where shadows twist to gibing fears?

"Lo, on this night the pestful devil foil!
Here is a lanthorn filled with soothing oil:
    With Me make thine abode,
  And I will thy red crimes assoil."

My heart is tired, I have not strength to moan,
I am so weak, my pride is overthrown—
    The pride which was my goad:
  My Lord, my God, I am Thine Own.

WHEAT AND CLOVER.

In a flower-strown lane where the bees were humming,
And a breath of limes in the calm hot air,
Through the wheat and clover I saw her coming,
And close together we wandered there.

    Some dear little birds in a tree
    Sang a wild song of delight;
    Sang a sweet song to my love and me,
While the sunshine danced and the day was bright.

On a white still beach we went idly straying
In the splendour and drowse of the soft full moon,
And we took no heed of the words we were saying,
As we walked our last in the night's deep noon.

    The tide sighed over the sand,
    A scared gull cried from her nest,
    But we went on happily hand-in-hand,
Our souls serene and our hearts at rest.

I have died since my dearest came out of the clover
In the sleepy hush of that summer's day;
Or *she* has died, and all is over,
And I am stupid and bent and grey.

    Oh, the birds are dead in the tree,
    The winds no more laugh in my ears;
    And when my darling comes back to me
I cannot see her from blinding tears.

37

LAKE GLAMOUR.

WHEN night-birds leave their nest
    Sweet dews to sup,
From the lake's sheeny breast
    Moon waves splash up,
And rain-drops rock to rest
    In lily's cup;
While from the stars comes dripping scented light:
    Oh, good night!

When the hair of the water-maid
    Clings to the oar,
Till the dreaming moon, half afraid,
    Basketh no more;
When kelpies lurk in the shade,
    Craved by the shore;
And even the low twangling harp-notes *sound* white:
    My love, good night!

HYMN TO ST. DOMINICK.

WHEN Christ our Lord by ruthless men
  Was slain upon a tree,
He knew that He would rise again,
  O blessed Saint, in thee.

He knew that thou wouldst come to Spain,
  His noble harbinger;
And leaving pomp and courtly train,
  Teach mankind not to err.

To read His Gospels for the poor
  I wot thou wert not slack:
Thou brought'st His peace to every door,
  And soothed'st the hind's sore lack.

To sweet Saint Mary, wisest maid,
  We learned to tell our beads:
Each holy bead when it is prayed
  Plants one of virtue's seeds.

All errors which the devil planned
  In vain and fell despight,
Were scoured before thee like the sand
  On some bleak wintry night.

From all thy toil, in Heaven's Court
  Thou takest now thy rest;
With Christ our Lord thou dost consort—
  Thy head upon His breast.

And since thou hast so straitly trod,
  Yet grieved at sinner's cry,
And talkest in the ear of God,
  Our prayers up to thee hie.

Grant us Thy grace, O Lord of Hosts,
  The love of Christ Thy Son,
The peace which is the Holy Ghost's:
  O blessed Three in One !
                                Amen.

O my soft brown son ! sleep close—
Close to little mother yearning :
The dew-grass swings, and sweetly brings
All the warmth of its burning.
Hush ! the wet green bird
Was the only sound you heard :
    She is singing
    To your swinging,
Singing is the sad green bird.

Do you know what she is singing,
Singing in the silver light ?
Ah ! she hopes for you, and mopes
Lest you fall ill in God's sight :
Lest inside your cream-calm sleep
Certain ugly fairies creep ;
    Some bad feeling
    Cometh stealing
Through your eyelids to your sleep.

All the laughing good dream-fairies,
Fairies with soft chamois shoon,
Bring you gleams of blue star-beams
And a cool song from the moon !
And our dear Lord's Mother smiling
Saves you from the Old Man's wiling :
    He goes gliding
    From her chiding,
While she kisses pink eyes smiling.

GARDEN FANTASY.

Into my garden comes a butterfly,
Bearing to me a message from my dear ;—
A dainty rover flitting there and here,
And looking on the roses with a sigh :
Along the sunlight streaming from the sky
Comes gaily flaunting this fair chevalier,
And dances up without a sign of fear
To soothe my lover's whispers, by-and-by.

How grieved he is that he is far away,
How he will see me soon, because he must,
How much in courtly routs my face he misses :
All this my prankéd messenger doth say
Alight upon my fingers, while fine dust
Falls from his wings to mark my darling's kisses.

ON A DAY.

BLITHE little bird,
   Sing from your nest a new song!
A chaunt which tells the praises word by word
Of my dear love, and lurks the boughs among,
And in the springtide is the first sound heard,
   Blithe little bird!

   Offerings of flowers
   I bring to my dear at day's close;
For I have gathered them in fragrant hours,
The modest coloured violet, the wet rose,
And the proud lily I bring to dreaming bowers:
   Offerings of flowers.

   Soft pretty name
   On the trunks of the trees let me carve;
And I shall kiss the letters without shame
When for the kisses of her mouth I starve:
For sure to carve *thee* cannot great trees maim,
   Soft pretty name!

   Ah, laughing eyes,
   The day of the flowers is soon over:
The leaves which soothed thy name grow sere from
   sighs,
Above our heads harsh winter-time doth hover;
And then—and then perhaps our child-love dies:
   Ah, laughing eyes!

WEIRD, weird children, did you spy Her
As She crossed the market-place,
Did you mark when She drew nigher
With the sunshine in Her face;
Did you note the little baby who was nestled to Her
        breast,
And how all the folk She met
Knew She went to pay their debt,
And were joyous and at rest:
Violet ones with dreaming eyes,
Were you very still and wise?

Weird, weird children, did you listen
To Her prayers before the Mass;
Did you see the scald tears glisten
Ere Her dolour came to pass;
Did you hear Her choke with sobbing when Her wee
        child went away,—
From Her face the joy departed,
She was sick and broken-hearted,
And her hair was shot with grey:—
Rosebuds that our Lord embraces,
Did you wonder in your places?

Weird, weird children, was She weeping
When She went forth from the town?
Did your tiny hands go creeping
To Her poor head hanging down?
Were you oh! so very sorry as you toddled by her
        side?—
Though you really could not tell
Why the funny tear-drops fell
When your eyes were opened wide:
Tell me, blossoms without guile,
Do you think you made her smile?

SPRING.

LEAVES of the lilach mingle with the flowers
And silvery drops of rain sprent o'er the sod:
I dream away the soundless, soothing hours,
'Mid breezes straying from the Court of God.

A THICK wet night is falling on the sighing, lashing
    waters,
The ship is sorely straining and the loneliness is drear ;
We hearken for the voices of our little sons and
    daughters,
Who are praying in a small grey village far away from
    here.

Mary, Star of the Sea,
Queen of the waves and the foam,
When the night-wrack is creeping, we softly ask Thee
To bring the poor mariner home.

Sometimes we cannot hear the hymns the little ones
    are singing,
But in the shrouds is crying, and a wailing sad and thin,
And then we know our Blessed Lady's gentle hands
    are wringing
For someone in the ship who has that day done mortal
    sin.

Queen of the winds and the rain,
Queen of the storm and the blast,
'Mid the shrieks in the rigging we beg Thee again,
To grant us Thy peace, at the last.

The night is very dark and the winds are hoarsely
    squalling,
The vessel moans and creaks as she threshes through
    the sea ;
But thank God ! we hear the voice of the Virgin Mary
    calling,
That She is here to guide us and to help to lead us free.

Queen in the High Heaven crowned,
Through the pains of our Lord on the Cross,
Have pity upon the poor folk that are drowned,
Whose corpses along the tide toss.

THE STATUE OF S. VINCENT DE PAUL IN AMIENS CATHEDRAL.

BECAUSE thou wert so gentle and so mild,
The children played and laughed about thy feet ;
Thy face with holy innocence was sweet,
Because thou wert as simple as a child—
Thy life as stainless and as undefiled :
In foul ways didst thou labour, yet the street
Nor fouled nor grimed thee ; and a sore defeat
Didst deal black sin which weakling men beguiled.

Lowly thou wert, and yet thou hast a place
In this majestic monument of years,
Thine eyes upon our Saviour and His Cross :
And sinners who have fallen far from grace,
Because thou art so meek bring thee their tears,
And crave thy prayers for ruth from direful loss.

BRETON LULLABY.

SLEEP, little baby with deep blue eyes,
Little fair baby whose soul is white ;
The hymns of the saints and good angels' sighs
Drowsily murmur round thee to-night :
Sleep, while the merry stars twinkle and gleam,
Sleep on thy pillow and prettily dream
Of the playing gold fishes that dart through the stream,
Till the angels awake thee at morning.

Dream, little baby, of launching a boat
Where tiny waves splash on the whispering sand :
O'er silent and silvery sea you float
Through the star-shine into the golden land.
Dream of a romp in a moonlit dell,
Where soft laughing fairies and nixies dwell,
While mother is watching to keep thee well,
Till the angels awake thee at morning.

Baby, my baby, life's ocean is grey,
The sun seldom shines and the storms are dread ;
That Jesus' Sweet Mother may guide thee I pray,
For this little mother will soon be dead.
Keep then, my darling, thy gentle soul white—
Pure as it is in thy slumber to-night,
And thy face shall be fair with the flash of God's light,
When the angels awake thee at morning.

HYMN TO OUR LADY OF PEACE.

O SWEETEST Marie, Queen of Peace,
Gain us from Christ Thy Son,
That comfort which, our hearts to ease,
He left as benison.

This world cannot give us quell,
'Tis such a wily place;
Thy holy peace will only dwell
In hearts a-fire with grace.

O dearest Maid, give me respect
For men who o'er me rise,—
Towards those with worldly honour decked
To act in peaceful wise.

The crowds of men who like me seem,
And are my equals hight,
Let me in truth my equals deem,
And love with all my might.

The men below me in degree
(I wot they are but few !)
May I not treat with vanity,
But yield to each his due:

And win the peace of God most High,
Ere yet it be too late;
And wail past sins with groan and sigh,
Do well in my estate.

Thy peace to good folk grant alway,
And to poor sinners even,
So they can feel, one blissful day,
The gracious peace of Heaven.

O sweetest Lady, Queen of Peace,
From foes and evil blight,
From all the plagues which mankind seize,
Protect us day and night.

Amen.

THE ANGELUS.

Dong! Dong! Dong!
In the calm of the evening sun
Softly tolls the Angelus;
All the stuff our staves have spun
Bless, O Mother Glorious!
Now the good old *curé* pauses
At the corner of the street,
Now Lucille standeth still
With her lover in the wheat.

The angel of the Lord came down
To a far-off Jewry town,
Where dwelt a maiden blest:
Jesus, friend of little children,
Give my baby rest.

Dong! Dong! Dong!
Damozels with faltering feet
Linger by the wayside cross,
And Our Lord they gently greet,
Asking ruth from final loss:
'Mid the shadows by the fountain,
In a silence that's a sound,
Poor Margot writeth slow
With her finger on the ground.

" Behold the handmaid of the Lord,
Be it done as His Own Word,"—
Thus spake white maid Marie:
Queen of all the Angel host,
I pray gramercy.

Dong! Dong! Dong!
Little children cease their play
When the holy bell they hear,
And in wondering whispers pray,
For to them God is so near.
By her son's grave in the churchyard,
Clasping one dead violet,
In the wind, weak and blind,
Mother Hortense weepeth yet.

Pour forth into our hearts Thy grace,
That we may run a goodly race
O Lord Who rulest above!
And through the suffering of Thy Son,
Shine in Thy Realm of Love.

WIDOW'S CROON.

Sleep, little clover, sleep!
A bad wind roughens the sea to-night,
And the blackness cannot lie close to the main;
I see, like a speck, a far vessel's light,
Through the gusts of the gale and the flaws of rain.
Oh, the power of God on the deep!
Sleep, little clover, sleep.

Sleep, little clover, sleep!
For foolish folk say that drowned men walk
In the trail of the storm the night-hags ride;
But mother is here, and the good Saints talk,
And thy Angel Guardian is at thy side.
Oh, the power of God on the deep!
Sleep, little clover, sleep.

Sleep, little clover, sleep!
When Our Lord comes down on that last great day,
And Queen Mary with stars in her shining hair,
The sailors who are tired of being dead will be gay,
And poor drowned father will sure be there.
Oh, the power of God on the deep!
Sleep, little clover, sleep.

THE END OF YEARS.

PERCHANCE, that morning in the sun,
The flowers will laugh and kiss the wind,
And blossoms open one by one,
While he is leaving all behind,

Who listless on his pillow turns,
And slowly shifts his waning gaze ;
For now the hour is when he learns
The secret of his baffled days.

And as a child when very tired
Goes happy with its nurse to bed,
So he too rest has long desired,
And follows to the patient dead.

How little time he was away !
How few the hours since he had birth
And huddled in a cot !—to-day
He lays his weary head in earth.

So for the world this is the end.
Whether he slaved or took his ease,
Beleaguered Truth, betrayed his friend—
No matter : now he is at peace.

And sleeps ?—ah ! one night he must wake,
And stand in an enormous plain
Amongst the dead, who writhe and shake
To see their buried lives again.

If man's life is a monument
Built from the stones of noble years,
Then shall he see the life he spent
Re-edified, with shameful tears.

At that time, God of heavenly Powers !
Take pity on our misery ;
Yea ! pity those poor eyes of ours,—
Poor eyes that would, but could not see.

WHEN the dark is thick, at the foot of my bed she
    stands,
With the sorrow around her mouth, and the eyes that
    linger and ache;
And she shadowly beckons to me with thin pale hands,
To come from the feverish hours that jeer through the
    darkness they shake:
And the hours fall away in sallow menacing bands,
As softly I drift into sleep, and sleeping still dream that
    I wake.

Through a mountain-pass I wind, in a desolate crowd
Of men and women, with hungry faces whipped and
    smeared by the rain,
Who murmur together, in voices not low nor loud,
Always the same stark words, slack-lipped and sore
    weeping from grinding pain:
On they stagger with hands a-tremble and poor heads
    bowed;
And I stagger after the hearse in step with this funeral
    train.

Ah, that sick pause!—The coffin falls down and blocks
    the way:
On the wreaths the frost-dew turns to blood and drips
    on the road dark red:
A monstrous corpse rolls out on the road in full display,
And the storm advances over the hills with thundering
    feet and dread:
While there (dear God!) in the sight of all—unshapen,
    grey,
Lies the glaring corpse of a human soul—my own bad
    soul, now dead.

Awake in the stifling dark, still I dream that I sleep:
Once more across my bed the hours sneer by, dragging
    with them the years ;
Hot fingers of old crimes about my stiff eye-lids creep,
And all night long before my wearied gaze triumph a
    thousand fears :
And lo ! the dream-wraith has faded, and fading did
    weep,—
Heart-tired for my sad sake, and left my pillow cold
    from her hot tears.

THE VEIL OF LIGHT.

HERE, where the vague winds, tired, come to sleep,
Here, where they hide when hunted by the rain ;
From this point whence the world looks far and deep,
We gaze triumphant on the earth's dull plain.

How hardly won !—but now this comely peace :
Even the sea-tang in the mellow air
Breathes harshly, and its strength disturbs the ease
Of yon thin cloud soft falling from God's Hair.

Ah, that bright cloud !—a curtain from the sky ;
That shifting filmy thing, that drifting gauze :
The dooms that 'neath its trembling shadows lie,
Though suns be in our hearts, must give us pause.

All down the valleys of the universe,
Through firmaments to where the tall stars end,
The terror lurks, and stabs us like a curse,
Whom Fear binds close together, O my friend !

Blank dreams are there that make a mock of life ;
And all of sinister that round the bed
Crawl in dark hours, alive and wet with strife ;
And all the thoughts when no more words are said.

And what unknown is there to mar our way ?
What more, O Blessèd Lord ! what vile thing more
Lies hid behind that mass of whitened grey ?
What furtive venom is there still in store ?

Hear, in Thy lofty place, Thy children calling !
Dead leaves, we ride upon the wings of night :
Remove, Lord God most High, this shroud appalling—
This hard, intolerable Veil of Light !

In the convent chapel the solemn tone
Of the vesper cadences rose and fell;
But the shadow cast over the altar-stone
By the night-fall, clouded my heart as well:
For with clang that deadened the organ's swell,
And the blithe-voiced quiresters' chaunt of trust,
By Doubt and Sorrow was knolled this knell:
Ashes to ashes, and dust to dust.

To the king who rules from a carven throne,
To the starveling folk who in hovels dwell,
To the dimpled maid, and the wrinkled crone,
This terrible tolling doth death foretell:
For the rich it throbs like a passing-bell,
For the haggard wretch who gnaws at a crust
It murmurs like soothing of soft sea-shell:
Ashes to ashes, and dust to dust.

The lorewise scholar who dreameth alone,
The pallid nun locked in her sombre cell,
The madmen who mutter, and mouth, and moan,
The hollow-eyed trulls with their souls to sell,—
Close their ears in vain to this warning fell;
For alike at wisdom, and prayer, and lust,
The Devil outlaughs from the end of Hell:
Ashes to ashes, and dust to dust.

Envoi.

O my God, shall Death this foul terror quell?—
Or when worms have battened on legs and bust,
Shall the *skull* give forth this atrocious yell?—
Ashes to ashes, and dust to dust!

TRANSLATIONS.

(*In the original metres.*)

DREAMYLAND.

(From Xanrof.)

On a white pillow covered with loveliest things,
In his warm, soft nightgown the little one sleeps ;
His Angel spreads gently his white, pearly wings,
And all black dreams away from the little cot keeps.
No thought of the future now troubles his head,
He's so tiny and weak he cannot understand.

      Sleep, sleep, baby sleep !
     Baby sleep in thy trundle-bed !
      Sleep, sleep, baby sleep !
    The wee one laughs in dreamyland.

By the side of his bed sits his mother who dreams
Of saving her child from all griefs that are ours,—
All sinning, and sorrow, and hot, blighting beams,—
" May his life-path be ever sprent over with flowers ! "
While he smiles in his sleeping and drowsily crows,
From her wist eyes she prays Time to lift off the band.

      Sleep, sleep, baby sleep !
    The lamp-shade makes thy face a rose ;
      Sleep, sleep, baby sleep !
    The wee one laughs in dreamyland.

When her child is a man, a beautiful head
One night will his pillow of lilies divide :
Then purely he'll kiss the fair dame he has wed
When he rises, or when he lies down by her side :
Together these two become whiter than snow,
Then one by himself must his burthen withstand.

Sleep, sleep, baby sleep !
The trembling light is burning low ;
Sleep, sleep, baby sleep !
The wee one laughs in dreamyland.

A greybeard lies dying, quite tired and old,
So tired that he wishes to sleep for alway :
One flower brings back warmth, and he is so cold !
One halo enlivens the wane of his day ;
On the lips of the old man a smile plays about,
As he looks at a cradle, and waves his thin hand.

Sleep, sleep, baby sleep !
Alack, the light has flickered out !
Sleep, sleep, baby sleep !
The wee one laughs in dreamyland.

PALENESS.

(*From François Coppée.*)

At eve used I frequently meet
That poorly-clad, radiant girl,
While there waited close by in the street
Some old blade—his bad mind in a whirl!
Scarce sixteen, yet so evilly wise,
And meeting men's eyes without quail;
But that hair, those teeth, and *such* eyes! . . .
And oh, so prettily pale!

I saw her again at the play,—
O'er three lovers she ruled like a queen;
I was dazed by the scintillant ray
Of her jewels with shimmering sheen.
Despite her look tired and acerb,
And deep eyes which told a wild tale . . .
How lovely she was—how superb!
And pale—so splendidly pale!

Alas! I chanced on my fair
In a dead-house but yesterday:
In the sunlight's pitiless glare,
Her corpse shewed thinly and grey.
And still her face, stiffened and cold,
Kept the choke when her breath did fail—
'Mid a cloud of the hair of gold . . .
Great God!—she was hatefully pale!

RHYMES.
(*From Alfred Poussin.*)

REPOS.

IF we are happy asleep in bed,
It must be exquisite to be dead.

UN MATIN DE PÂQUE.

THROUGHOUT the Lent just passed away
I've fasted till I'm starved and beat;
Here's Easter—now, this very day!
But I've not got a thing to eat.

À UNE JEUNE FILLE.

IF by some grace divine I did inherit
Cellini's art or Buonarruoti's own,
Then shouldst thou live, a white and gladsome spirit,
For ever in the magic carven stone.

LE SILENCE D'OR.

MY Lord, of all the wealth that's by you holden,
I asked a pound to help me from this rut;
But well you knew that silence is deemed golden,
And so you kept your mouth and purse-clasp shut.

RÉVOLTE.

RUINED by ills, man shudders to the core:
But when the death-blow brings him to the sod
He turns about, and shakes his fist at God,
Yelling in fury:—"Strike me, Thou, once more!"

MA STATUE.

I AM a poet, and you shall find my statue
At Dunkerque, as a saint of ancientry:
One favour let me ask,—'tis simple: That you,
When you kneel at your prayers, remember me.

LA DESTRUCTION.
(*From Charles Baudelaire.*)

THE Devil stirs about me without rest,
And round me floats like noxious air and thin;
I breathe this poison-air which scalds my breast,
And fills me with desires of monstrous sin.

Knowing my love of Art, he sometimes takes
The shape of supple girls supremely fair;
And with a wily, canting lie he makes
My heated lips his shameful potions share.

Then far he leads me from the sight of God,
Crushed with fatigue, to where no man has trod—
To the vague, barren plains where silence sounds,

And hurls into my face his foul construction
Of slimy clothes, and gaping, putrid wounds,
And all the bleeding harness of Destruction!

CHISWICK PRESS:—CHARLES WHITTINGHAM AND CO.
TOOKS COURT, CHANCERY LANE, LONDON.